NATHAN MAYNARD is a Trawlwoolway man and multidisciplinary artist from Larapuna country, Lutrawita/Tasmania.

Nathan has been a practicing artist for the best part of 25 years, firstly exploring his creative instincts through cultural and contemporary dance before finding theatre in 2013, acting in the Terrapin Puppet Theatre production, *Shadow Dreams*. Since then, Nathan has written seven full length plays, including *The Season*, *At What Cost*, *A Not So Traditional Story* and *Hide The Dog*, which he co-wrote with acclaimed Maori writer and performer Jamie McCaskill. Nathan's plays have been performed nationally on some of Australia's biggest stages, including the Sydney Opera House's Drama Theatre. Nathan also performed in Terrapin Puppet Theatre's production of his play, *A Not So Traditional Story*, notching up over 200 performances along the way. Nathan directed the 2019 Junction Festival production, *Journey of The Free Words*, Melbourne Art Play's production of Nazaree Dickerson's play *Crumbs* and the 2022 Jute Theatre's remount tour production of Isaac Drandić's *Back on Track*. Nathan assistant-directed the 2022 Belvoir Street Theatre production of his play, *At What Cost*. In 2024, Nathan directed Mudlark Theatre Company's critically acclaimed production of *The Box*, which Nathan also co-wrote with Murri writer and comedian, Rob Braslin.

37

NATHAN MAYNARD

CURRENCY PRESS
The performing arts publisher

CURRENCY PLAYS

First published in 2024
by Currency Press Pty Ltd,
Gadigal Land, Suite 310, 46–56 Kippax Street, Surry Hills, NSW 2010, Australia
enquiries@currency.com.au
www.currency.com.au

in association with Melbourne Theatre Company

This revised edition first published in 2025.

Typeset by Brighton Gray for Currency Press.
Cover design by Mathias Johansson for Currency Press.

Currency Press acknowledges the Traditional Owners of the Country on which we live and work. We pay our respects to all Aboriginal and Torres Strait Islander Elders, past and present.

Contents

Disclaimer: Please note the following introduction contains major spoilers for 37. *If you have not yet seen or read the play, we recommend reading the introduction after finishing the script.*

37 was commissioned and developed through Melbourne Theatre Company's NEXT STAGE Writers' Program.

Melbourne Theatre Company acknowledges the Boon Wurrung and Wurundjeri Woi Wurrung peoples of the Kulin Nation, the traditional custodians of the land on which we work, create and gather. We pay our respects to all First Nations people, their Elders past and present, and their enduring connections to Country, knowledge, and stories. As a Company we remain committed to the invitation of the Uluru Statement from the Heart and its call for voice, truth and treaty.

Introduction: 'Accepted rules' and the un-Australian

The game of Australian Rules Football is a beautiful thing. Its origins came from the traditional Aboriginal game called Marngrook, where the athleticism and skill displayed is second to no other sport in the world. Marngrook is like traditional Aboriginal dance and ballet fused together in graceful harmony. Then there's the physicality and the camaraderie. The friendships that are formed when humans go into battle with one another are lifelong. Race, politics or class eventually do not matter. If you wear the same colours and you sing the same song, you are one of the pack. You are accepted. You are meant to belong.

Aboriginal players have made a significant contribution to the game of Australian Rules Football. Many players have been central to the success of their aligned clubs, displaying skills never seen before on a footy field. They have been celebrated in ways that Aboriginal people had never been celebrated before, honoured with adornments, medallions and respect from teammates and footy-loving fans for a moment in time.

Some players even changed the way the modern-day game is played. I think of the Krakouer brothers who had an uncanny ability to find one another on the field no matter how dense the pack; who, with quick successive handballs, broke through defensive lines with their run and carry, revolutionising the game's strategies.

Then there are players like Chris Lewis and Nicky Winmar who challenged the behavioural standards in the AFL in the 1980s and 1990s. Both players were subject to abhorrent racism throughout their entire careers. Despite the racism they endured, they are amongst some of the best to have ever played the game. You might remember the image of Nicky Winmar lifting his St Kilda guernsey, pointing to his black skin and shouting to the Collingwood crowd, 'I'm black and I'm proud!' This iconic image etched its way into the minds of football-loving Australians forever. It was a turning point in the AFL.

Racial vilification was now on the AFL's agenda, and they began developing behavioural standards that would be implemented across the professional competition and through to the amateur and junior leagues. From this point onwards, the AFL and Aboriginal players have done more for this country in combating racism than many other organisations — including, one might say, the Australian government. They continue to lead the way.

However, there is always more learning to do. Specifically, more that should have been done to protect Indigenous player Adam Goodes during the last years of his AFL career. Adam was subject to constant booing and taunts by fans and media in the most public and enduring display of racism ever seen in the professional sporting arena in Australia. The AFL should have intervened earlier.

37, named after the guernsey number immortalised by Adam Goodes, centres an amateur country football club, the Cutting Cove Currawongs, during the era of Goodes' famous 'War Cry' dance. In an AFL match against Carlton, during the 2015 Sir Doug Nicholls Round (an annual AFL event instilled with the explicit purpose of celebrating Indigenous culture), Goodes celebrated after kicking a goal by dancing and shaking an imaginary spear towards the opposition crowd. This act of celebrating his culture with a traditional Aboriginal dance sent the media—more so than the Carlton supporters—into a frenzy that encouraged Australia's racism to, once again, rear its ugly head. Goodes' celebration dance was seen as an act of aggression. It was seen as un-Australian because it did not fit within the 'accepted rules' of Aboriginal expression. It was such a disappointing time for the AFL and for Aboriginal people, after working so hard to erase racism from our national sport.

What Nathan Maynard brings to our attention in *37* is that, when an Aboriginal person 'steps out of line' and does something outside of the 'accepted rules', they become an easy target for the greater structural evil of racism in this country. Sonny and Jayma, the two talented Aboriginal cousins who join the Cutting Cove Currawongs, represent both those who bite their tongue to protect themselves within a hostile space, and those who will receive violence when they choose to speak up. When Jayma steps up and expresses his support of Goodes' dance, he becomes a target for vilification in the football club. He goes from being loved and celebrated by the team, the club and their fans, to being subjected to anti-social and downright racist behaviour:

> JOE: Mate, I love ya, but you just can't leave things be.
>
> WOODSY: Watch out Joe, the sook will call you a racist next … Does anybody else notice we never see Sonny calling us all white cunts or fighting with anybody?
>
> DAZZA: Because he's easygoing, our Sonny.
>
> SONNY: No, because look what happens when you bite back. You did all leave Jayma to dry out there today, and he's right, it was because the young warrior stood up to you.
>
> WOODSY: 'Warrior', what a joke! Your people aren't warriors, warriors don't lose. Your people lost to our people and you need to get over it. Simple.

The victories of Indigenous athletes will be upheld as virtues of the nation, while the personal freedoms and rights to expression for Indigenous individuals will be dismissed. The team's awkward shunning of Jayma is the beginning of the end for the Cutting Cove Currawongs. No longer does Jayma want to 'put his body on the line' and win games of football—off his own boot —for a team and a club that considers having an opinion different to the white majority as 'stepping out of line'.

Thanks to Jayma's initial contributions, the Cutting Cove Currawongs go on to play in the grand final after their decades-long curse of being at the bottom of the ranks. They have a chance to win the ultimate prize in football, the holy grail, to drink 'the angel piss' from the premiership cup, but without unity amongst the team there is no way they can achieve this Australian dream. All that hard work to get to the grand final is undone. All that potential to be something great wasted. We're left with the question: 'What could have been? What could this club have looked like if only … ?' And for those of you who are searching for deeper meaning, what could Australia look like, if we didn't act like this? Unfortunately, in the play, we'll never know. Perhaps in real life we will one day. One would hope we've learnt from this time.

Years on from Goodes' retirement, the CEO of the AFL (at the time) Gillon McLachlan finally admitted the AFL should have called out the booing as racism. 'In the end there's a point where you've just got to call it,' McLachlan said. 'We were too nuanced in trying to manage too many people to an outcome instead of just being really clear and calling it out and letting the cards fall after that.'

Managing 'too many people to an outcome' came at the cost of an exceptionally gifted athlete who advocated for his people's right to justice in this country. In the duration of his career, Goodes was a dual Brownlow medallist, two-time premiership player, four-time All Australian, three-time club champion, member of the Indigenous Team of the Century and Australian of the Year (2014). The list goes on. Goodes has not engaged with the AFL in any capacity since his retirement. Too little too late, it seems.

It makes you wonder: if an Australian of the Year can be the punching bag for a nation of racists, take a minute to think about all the Aboriginal people who don't have the profile and resume of this great man. Perhaps he was targeted because he was in a position of influence and power. Perhaps he challenged the popular perception of Aboriginal men in a way that shook Australians to the very core of their deep-seated racist foundations. What does it mean to denote our First Peoples as un-'Australian', as un-belonging? Ugly convictions rear their heads when we play a beautiful game that precedes this country's name.

Isaac Drandić
Director

The premiere professional production of *37* was first presented by Melbourne Theatre Company and Queensland Theatre at Southbank Theatre, The Sumner, Melbourne on the lands of the Boon Wurrung and Wurundjeri peoples of the Kulin Nation, on 2 March 2024, with the following cast and creatives:

THE GENERAL	Syd Brisbane
GORBY	Mitchell Brotz
APPLES	Samuel Buckley
ANT	Costa D'Angelo
GJ	Thomas Larkin
WOODSY	Eddie Orton
JOE	Ben O'Toole
JAYMA	Ngali Shaw
DAZZA	Anthony Standish
SONNY	Tibian Wyles

Director and Co-Choreographer, Isaac Drandić
Assistant Director, Kamarra Bell-Wykes
Set and Costume Designer, Dale Ferguson
Lighting Designer, Ben Hughes
Composer and Sound Designer, James Henry
Co-Choreographer, Waangenga Blanco
Voice and Text Coach, Matt Furlani
Fight Choreographer, Lyndall Grant
Intimacy Coordinator, Isabella Vadiveloo

A studio presentation of *37* took place at the Victorian College of the Arts [VCA], 18–22 October 2022, directed by Isaac Drandić and performed by the VCA Class of 2022, with Syd Brisbane. The cast included: Damon Baudin, Zacheriah Blampied, Samuel Buckley, Michael Cooper, Costa D'Angelo, Ben de Pagter, Will Hall, Harry McGee, Ethan Rutledge, Benjamin Smith, and Maximilian Wilson. The presentation featured Choreography by Jacob Boehme, Set Design by Leon Salom, Costume Design by Olivia Lucia Pimpinella, Lighting Design by Stephen Hawker, and Sound Design by Riley McCullagh. The VCA presentation was supported by Melbourne Theatre Company, The Vizard Foundation and the Faculty of Fine Arts and Music, University of Melbourne.

CHARACTERS

JAYMA, Aboriginal, the team's star player, 21, male.

SONNY, Aboriginal, a player and Jayma's big cousin, 27, male.

THE GENERAL, the team's coach, 55, male.

JOE, the team captain, 30, male.

DAZZA, player/trainer and club board member, 36, male.

APPLES, player, 20, male.

WOODSY, player, 28, male.

GORBY, player, 22, male.

GJ, player and coach's son, 22, male.

ANT, second-generation Italian-Australian, player, 24, male.

PROLOGUE: MARNGROOK BEGINNINGS

The ensemble play a culturally stylised game (or flashes of a game) of marngrook. It is traditional, flashy, smooth, graceful and eloquent. It has an organic and instinctual feel to it.

It is in contrast to the AFL football we see later, which is rough and militaristic in its style.

JAYMA *exits the game, finds his position on stage and begins to talk to the audience.*

JAYMA: Before an AFL football was kicked on this country, there were footballs kicked all around it, however, these footballs, they weren't AFL footies and they weren't made from cattle hides.

Nah.

The footballs I'm talking 'bout, they were made from reeds, from the kangaroo skins. And in Victoria, the birth place of AFL, they were made from possum skin and the mobs called this game *marngrook*.

Mobs played marngrook for hours, even days at a time. They'd drop punt that possum skin ball into the air and then before it'd hit the ground, someone would soar above the pack and mark it. And then it'd be that fulla's turn to drop it on their foot, and launch it back into the sky. There were sides, but it was played for joy, no scores kept, but with the ball launched into that sky as a token of friendship between mobs. And at the end of the day, those old fullas, they'd bury that ball into the ground, to say thank you to that country and that country would look after that ball until they played the game called marngrook again.

SCENE ONE: SEASON LAUNCH

The clubhouse.

The chanting voices of the TEAM *are accompanied by clapping.*

TEAM: The General, the General, the General, the General, the General, the General, the General …

Lights come up and we first see two massive currawongs etched into the walls of the clubhouse.

As the lights begin to gather in brightness, we make out a lectern and two long tables, which are occupied by men. There is an inaudible ruckus which is made from the collective voices that fill the space.

THE GENERAL *approaches the lectern.*

THE GENERAL: Okay, okay. Thank you, thank you! You fellas, and ladies, make an old man feel like a rock star. I can tell you I don't get this reception at home. At home, I'm lucky to be called in late for dinner.

Laughs in the room.

Who's excited about the season ahead?

TEAM: Woo woo!

THE GENERAL: I SAID: WHO'S EXCITED FOR A FRESH OPPORTUNITY?!

TEAM: WOO WOO!

THE GENERAL: I should launch our season by thanking those people who will make it possible. Starting with our sponsors. Wheatley's Windows. East Coast Coaches, Robbo's Auto Repairs and of course, Herrings IGA.

TEAM: Up the IGA!

THE GENERAL: They say a football club is the heartbeat of a country town and in our case, you community-minded angels are the pacemaker that keeps that heart ticking. Thank you!

Applause.

Our members. This year we've already sold two thousand, three hundred and forty-two memberships.

Applause.

And considering this stretch of coastline we live along only has a population of twenty-two thousand, this a monumental achievement.

Applause.

I'm pretty sure Ant's family brought two hundred of them.

Laughs.

This club didn't happen by accident! This great club that you all love, like a brother, an uncle, a father, like a mother. It didn't happen by itself. It was birthed by good honest people and it's kept alive by good honest people! The majority of those people being seventh generation coasters who will bleed for this club. And if they're not directly a part of the day to day running of the club, they're here every week rain, hail or shine, cheering our boys on. I swear most game days, the entire town of Cutting Cove is here. Cars squashed in like sardines around the oval. Grandstands packed to the rafters and a sodden-wet area that's already in full voice by first bounce with our town's finest.

I've lost count of the amount of times we've been deep in the trenches, backs to the wall, fighting to stay in a game when the ground erupts into ...

TEAM: [*waving their scarfs*] Black white we're all right! Black white we're all right! Black white we're all right!

THE GENERAL: And the majority of the time the boys, the boys ... respond to the town's chant and get us over the line.

TEAM: THE BOYS, THE BOYS, THE MIGHTY COVE BOYS!!!!

THE GENERAL: But there's an elephant in the room.

We are a proud strong club steeped in a long history and tradition and yet, we still haven't won a premiership. I won't beat around the bush, that statistic is a *stain* on this footy club.

It's not good enough being a proud club. We want to be a great club and great clubs win ...

EVERYONE: Premierships.

THE GENERAL: I took the helm of this football club three years ago with the promise I would deliver a flag by my fourth season. The time has come for me to deliver on that promise, for us to deliver on our promise to the town.

THE GENERAL *sniffs the air.*

I love that smell, that's more than the smell of a new footy season. That's the smell of hope and fresh opportunity.

This season, chances will be offered to us. And it's up to us, as a club, to clunk those opportunities.

TEAM: WOO!

SCENE TWO: GET ON THE BUS

SONNY: Nah, fuck that. I'm going back to Mangana.

> SONNY *goes to walk off.* JAYMA *grabs him.*

JAYMA: Don't be a soft cock. Get on the bus.

SONNY: Call me a soft cock again, you little cumstain, and I'll shove that ball up your arse.

JAYMA: Cuz, please, just jump on the bus with me.

SONNY: Jayma, I've got three youngins under five, a missus who's stressed to her earholes and there's a million and three things that have to be done around the house. The last thing I need is to go away, to a farm in buttfuck nowhere, with a bunch of white fellas I don't know, on a footy pre-season camp.

JAYMA: We'll get to know 'em.

SONNY: Jayma, you don't need me to go with you. Your dad did it by himself.

JAYMA: I'm not my dad, and that's a lot of white fellas to one black fella.

SONNY: They don't want an old cunt like me. They only signed me up to sure you up.

JAYMA: That's bullshit. You're a gun and you're twenty-eight, not thirty-eight.

SONNY: Yeah, that's old in footy. In this big flash coast league, they want young bucks that they can mould into their footy minions.

JAYMA: You're just scared that you won't make the cut.

SONNY: Who?

JAYMA: You. And then you won't be able to use the old excuse like the rest of 'em in Mangana.

'I could have made it to the coast league, if I wanted to, but I didn't wanna leave the valley and the mob.' So you're using your age as an excuse.

SONNY: Go fuck yourself.

JAYMA: Am I right?

SONNY: Fuck you. I was gunna try out for the Currawongs when I was your age, I hitchhiked down from the valley to the coast, but I chickened out last minute and hitchhiked back.

JAYMA: Well, see, this is ya second chance then! We'll smash out a pre-season, make sure we're in the starting team and then dominate like Dad did down here for them. And before you know it, they'll be erecting another grandstand in Mangana, and this time, they'll be naming it the 'Jayma and Sonny Grandstand'.

SONNY: Don't ever say the word 'erecting' and our names in the same sentence ever again.

JAYMA: You know what, take the piss, Sonny, but I've got dreams, okay? I wanna do something with my footy.

SONNY: So did I once upon a time. But I've got three shitty-arse younguns and a missus to worry about. And we're already broke as fuck, brah. Look, it's gunna cost at least a hundred bucks a week going back and forth from Mangana to the coast in fuel. I love footy, you know this. But I can play in the valley and it won't cost me a cent.

JAYMA: Yes, but they don't pay you eight hundred bucks in the valley, do they?

SONNY: You said it was two hundred bucks a game.

JAYMA: That's what I heard on the black vine but the General sent me an email and it said it was eight hundred bucks. At the minimum.

SONNY: You're pulling me dick?

JAYMA: *At the minimum.*

SONNY: Okay, that's good money, but you know what beats money?

JAYMA: Legend status.

SONNY: No, fuck ya. The marngrook, the love of the game. They're too serious, these coast league fuckers. There's no joy in what they do.

JAYMA: We'll take the marngrook to them. We'll gracefully carve their comp up with smiles on our black faces.

    Pause.

C'mon, let's get on the bus. Together. The marngrook cousins!

    Pause.

SONNY: I fucken hate you.

JAYMA: I fucken love you.

SONNY: For the marngrook.

JAYMA: For the marngrook.

SCENE THREE: VOICES, BOYS

The typical footy-training talk and sounds can be heard. The sounds of leather hitting hands. The sounds of bodies hitting the bag. The sounds of footy boots thudding into the grass underneath. The constant chatter of a footy training drill.

JOE: Sonny, Sonny!

APPLES: Yep, Skipper!

GJ: Apples, Apples.

THE GENERAL: Pick up the voices, boys!

WOODSY: GJAAAAAY!

ANT: On the tit, Woodsy!

GORBY: Yep, put it here, bruv.

JAYMA: Yep yep yep yep brus.

SONNY: Cuz, cuz, cuz, yep.

THE GENERAL: Names, Sonny, names, Jayma!

JOE: Apples, Apples.

APPLES: Here, here, Skip.

THE GENERAL: Pick up the pace lads.

GJ: Woodsy!

WOODSY: GJAAAYYY!

ANT: On the tit, Woodsy, on the titty!

GORBY: ANT MAN, ANT MAN!

JAYMA: Put it here, brah.

SONNY: Yeah bro.

THE GENERAL: Names lads!

JOE: Put her here, Sonny, Put her here!

APPLES: In the basket, Skipper!

DAZZA: Clean hands, boys!!

GJ: Right here, Apples.

WOODSY: GJAAAAYYY!

ANT: Woodsy, on the titty again, bruv, on the titty.

GORBY: Ant!!!!

JAYMA: Yes!!!!

DAZZA: Don't pat the thing, hit the bag!

JAYMA *accidently knocks* DAZZA *over whilst bumping the pad.*

Good work, boys. Grab a drink of water.

They all grab a drink and gather round in a circle.

GORBY: [*to* JAYMA] Mate, you are Ferrari quick!

ANT: Yeah, and as smooth as Nonno's vino.

APPLES: And as elegant your sister, Ant.

ANT *playfully slaps* APPLES *around the head.*

GJ: You're the package, mate.

APPLES: It was like watching Cyril Rioli.

JAYMA: Nah, I'm Adam Goodes, brah. He's Cyril.

WOODSY: You can be whoever you like. As long as you're both going to put in the work.

GORBY: Bruv, the General was frothing over you two.

THE GENERAL *enters.*

THE GENERAL: What's that translate to, Gorby?

GORBY: I better go and run a lap.

THE GENERAL: Make it two laps.

GORBY: Two laps.

GORBY *runs off.*

THE GENERAL: [*to* JAYMA *and* SONNY] How are you boys going?

JAYMA / SONNY: Alright.

THE GENERAL: Who are you bunking with?

JAYMA: Joe.

THE GENERAL: The Captain has taken you under his wing, good. And he's the tidiest of the lot of them, one could even loosely describe him as being hygienic.

SONNY: Who owns this farm, General?

THE GENERAL: Woodsy's family. They're good enough to let us have training camp here every year.

JAYMA: You reckon I can play in the guts, brah?

THE GENERAL *laughs.*

THE GENERAL: We'll see, lad. Now, I'm not meaning to ride you two about the names, but communication is pretty damn important on a football field.

SONNY: Yeah, we get it.

THE GENERAL: You fellas aren't related to the late great Darky Mansell from Mangana?

SONNY: You mean Cedric.

JAYMA: Yeah, he was my dad.

THE GENERAL: Of course he was, look at you.

THE GENERAL *sympathetically touches* JAYMA*'s shoulder.*

Geez, that man could play. I watched him when he came down from the valley to play for the Currawongs. I've never seen an individual season like it. He kicked ten from the middle in his first game, for Christ sakes.

If he had've showed up for the Grand Final, the Currawongs would have won the flag that year.

JAYMA: Well, let's win the flag this year.

THE GENERAL: So you want a flag?

JAYMA: That's the plan, General. To finish what my old man started.

THE GENERAL: Well, you're going to have to work for it.

JAYMA: We're not scared of a bit of work.

THE GENERAL: Good, because the hard yakka hasn't even started yet.

SCENE FOUR: PRE-SEASON

A continuation from the last scene.

EVERYONE *has a rest for a moment.*

JOE: Hey, marngrook cousins, a few of the lads are going on a little adventure up to the top paddock tonight. It's a bit of a club tradition. You two should come along.

JAYMA: I'm in.

SONNY: Yeah, why not.

JOE: Great.

WOODSY *makes his way to* JAYMA.

WOODSY: You're a cheeky one aren't you, mate.

JAYMA: What?

WOODSY: You've been here for two minutes and you're asking the General if you can play in the guts.

JAYMA: Settle petal, there's room for us both.

JAYMA *turns his back on* WOODSY.

SONNY: [*to* JAYMA] Nina nayri? [You okay?]
JAYMA: Muna. [Yeah.]

JAYMA *and* SONNY *share a laugh.*

WOODSY: We speak English at this club, fellas.
THE GENERAL: Okay, partner up with the teammate next to you and give me ten chest-bumps … Now!

JAYMA *and* WOODSY *are forced to do the exercise together.*

TEAM: ONE, TWO, THREE, FOUR, FIVE, SIX, SEVEN, EIGHT, NINE, TEN.

DAZZA *blows a whistle for them to repeat the drill.*

ONE, TWO, THREE, FOUR, FIVE, SIX, SEVEN, EIGHT, NINE, TEN!

DAZZA *blows the whistle again.*

ONE, TWO, THREE, FOUR, FIVE, SIX, SEVEN, EIGHT, NINE, TEN!

The players other than JAYMA *and* WOODSY *fall in a heap with exhaustion.*

JAYMA *and* WOODSY *don't stop.*

JAYMA / WOODSY: ONE, TWO, THREE, FOUR, FIVE, SIX, SEVEN, EIGHT, NINE, TEN!
THE GENERAL: Okay, you two can let go of each other's hands now.
JAYMA: [*suggesting they're soft*] You moisturise?
WOODSY: Get fucked, dickhead.
JAYMA: [*sniffing his hand*] Vanilla bean.
THE GENERAL: Okay, give me two lines. We're not finished yet.

The TEAM *sighs.*

DAZZA: Dry your eyes, ladies.
APPLES: It's alright for you, you lazy bastard, Dazza!
DAZZA: I'm not lazy! Training is difficult for me, I have / genetically tight hamstrings.

EVERYONE: Genetically tight hamstrings.

APPLES: What are we doing now, General?

THE GENERAL: Your favourite, Apples.

APPLES: It's not really my favourite, is it?

THE GENERAL: No. It's the seated hip-walk race. The team who wins, gets out of the next drill.

GJ: The next drill?

THE GENERAL: Yes, the next drill, Junior. Have you got a problem with that?

GJ: …

THE GENERAL: Good.

Ready, set …

> DAZZA *blows a whistle to start. They race. It's loud and fun. The team* JAYMA *is in finishes second. The winning team celebrate accordingly.*

Winners take a seat, losers on your feet.

JAYMA: The boys are fucked, unc.

DAZZA: Oh, have a sook, ya fucken sook.

THE GENERAL: Tell you what. You beat me in a game of 'Taps Behind the Knee', Jayma, you get your team out of the drill.

WOODSY: And if he doesn't beat you?

THE GENERAL: You have to do it twice.

DAZZA: Take him, Jayma!

JOE: Kick his old fossilised arse, Jayma.

WOODSY: I'm not doing it twice if he loses.

THE GENERAL: Oh yes you will, Woodsy, because the team always comes …

TEAM: FIRST!

THE GENERAL: AND?

TEAM: SECOND!

THE GENERAL: AND?

TEAM: THIRD!

THE GENERAL: Bring it on, boy.

JAYMA: Bring it on, old man.

> JAYMA *and* THE GENERAL *take up wrestling postures.*
>
> *They begin playing 'Taps Behind the Knee'.*

They swing, dodge and weave. The rest of the TEAM *cheering on their fancy. The game going for as long as it needs to go for, before,* THE GENERAL *taps the back of* JAYMA*'s knee and becomes the winner.*

THE GENERAL*'s supporters are cheering and* JAYMA*'s teammates are sighing.*

WOODSY: I could see that coming a mile away!

JOE: Yeah, well there's no use crying about it. Let's go. We're a team.

They break into exercise. THE GENERAL *joins them*

JAYMA / JOE / SONNY / WOODSY / THE GENERAL: ONE, TWO, THREE, FOUR! ONE TWO THREE! ONE TWO! ONE!
ONE, TWO, THREE, FOUR! ONE TWO THREE! ONE TWO! ONE!
ONE, TWO, THREE, FOUR! ONE TWO THREE! ONE TWO! ONE!

THE GENERAL: Okay hill sprints now! Let's go! Knees up, knees up, knees up!

The boys run off, followed by THE GENERAL.

SCENE FIVE: MOO!

A paddock on Woodsy's property.

Hiding away from the coaches on the pre-season camp. They're passing around a whiskey bottle and a joint.

GORBY: It's as cold as a stiffy in a morgue.

WOODSY: Youse didn't let my cows out of the paddocks, did you?

GORBY: Fuck your cows, it's the General I'm worried about.

ANT: I reckon the General knows what's going on anyway, boys.

JOE: GJ, does he?

GJ: I dunno?

WOODSY: You didn't snitch on us?

GJ: Why would I snitch?

WOODSY: 'Cause he's your daddy.

GJ: Oh yeah: 'Hey Daddy, I'm going to smoke a joint with the boys' … makes heaps of sense. I'd be more worried about Dazza.

DAZZA: General Junior, I'm a joker, I'm a smoker, I'm the original motherfucking midnight toker.

GORBY: GJ, what was it like growing up with the General as your dad?

GJ: Normal, because you don't know any different.

APPLES: You didn't have to run laps if you forgot to empty the rubbish?

GJ: You don't forget to empty the rubbish in the General's household.

JOE: Did you ever see him play footy?

GJ: Only the once.

JOE: Did he dominate?

GJ: [*hesitantly*] Fuck yeah.

ANT: You can tell he was a gun just by the way he moves.

SONNY: What did he do before he became a coach?

GJ: He was headmaster.

ANT: At your school?

GJ: Yep.

GORBY: That'd suck dog's cock.

APPLES: It's dog's balls, you cretin.

> *They all laugh.*

JOE: Where'd you get this smoke from, Ant, that is on point, mate.

ANT: I confiscated it from a couple of teenagers at the shopping centre.

GORBY: You arsehole!

ANT: Hey, I could've made a big deal about it and got their parents involved, they would have copped a fucken schiaffo. But you know what, they get away with a warning and we get a free smoke. Everyone is happy … that's good country security-guarding, boys.

SONNY: You're a mall cop?

APPLES: More like a mafioso.

ANT: That's right, 'I made them an offer they couldn't refuse.'

GORBY: Ha, look at Jayma's face, he's tripping dog's balls … or is it cocks. Fuck, you have me all confused now, you cunts.

> EVERYONE *laughs.*

JOE: How you going there, Jayma?

JAYMA: I'm all good, brus, just sore.

ANT: I'm with you, bruv, it's my quads.

JOE: I struggled to get my shoes on earlier.

GORBY: You wear Crocs, you old bastard.

JOE: And that's how sore I am, smartarse. Couldn't even slip into my
    Crocs without a yelp.

> WOODSY *has a couple of tokes and passes the joint on to* JAYMA.
> JAYMA *has a toke and coughs his lungs up.*

APPLES: It's 'cause you're old, Skip.
WOODSY: You nearly ready to hang the boots up, aye, Captain?
JOE: Not without a flag!
JAYMA: You've never won a flag?
JOE: Nut, not in twenty-five years of playing footy.
    But that's gunna change this season, I can feel it in my waters.
APPLES: Do men have waters, Skipper?
JOE: What kind of skipper would I be with no waters, Apples?
JAYMA: Why do you feel it in those waters?
JOE: Because it's been building over the last three years.
GORBY: Since the General came to the club.
JOE: The season before the General, we came dead last. Not third last,
    not second last, we came …
EVERYONE: [*not* JAYMA *or* SONNY] Dead fucken last.
JOE: We were shells of what you see before you now. Empty footballing
    souls. Just cannon fodder for the teams above us. Which was every
    team, because we came …
EVERYONE: [*not* JAYMA *or* SONNY] Dead fucken last.
JOE: And since then, every year we have made steady progress and
    every year our belief has grown with it. And that's because of the
    General. He's been to the top, he knows the path. He's a master
    tactician, a master teacher and he has a way of making you believe.
    Three years ago, we were …
EVERYONE: [*not* JAYMA *or* SONNY] Dead fucken last!
JOE: And last year we were this close to making it to the big dance.
    Lost the prelim final by a kick to the team that ended up going on
    to win the flag. But to be honest, we've been missing that X-factor
    that takes a good team and turns it into a premiership team … and
    here you two are.
SONNY: Here we are.
JOE: Everyone in town says your old man was a freak and if he had've
    played in that Grand Final, the Currawongs would have won a flag
    that year.

GJ: Why was he a no-show, Jayma?

JAYMA: I dunno, but I wanna finish his dream. I wanna win that flag for him.

JOE: Let's do it. United forces on a mission to reach the one goal. Glory! Fuck, I can feel it!

APPLES: And we haven't even started yet.

JOE: And we haven't even started yet, Apples.

> WOODSY *gives* JOE *a knowing look*

But before we can start, something must happen.

WOODSY: Tradition must happen.

ANT: A Cutting Cove Currawongs tradition.

JOE: Since the inception of our footy club, new players must prove their allegiance to our club. An allegiance to its past players, current players, and to the cause of premiership success!

GORBY: Sonny looks nervous as fuck.

SONNY: 'Cause I am nervous as fuck.

> EVERYONE *laughs.*

JOE: *And*, the new bucks must prove their allegiance to our mighty footy club by the way of …

EVERYONE: [*not* JAYMA *or* SONNY] FINGER IN THE BOVINE SPHINCTER! FINGER IN THE BOVINE SPHINCTER! FINGER IN THE BOVINE SPHINCTER!

SONNY: No, no, no.

JOE: Yes yes, yes, my man.

JAYMA: Wait, whatta we doing?

SONNY: We have to stick a finger up a cow's arse.

ANT: That cow over there to be specific.

COW: [*offstage*] Moo!

JAYMA: No, no, no

EVERYONE: Yes, yes, yes.

SONNY: A finger, as in one finger?

JOE: The one digit, yes.

SONNY: Look after your elders and take one for the team, little cuz.

JAYMA: You're not pulling this 'elder card' here, brah. No way!

> SONNY *pretends to pull an 'elder card'.*

SONNY: Fucken oath I am!

JOE: As much as I'm enjoy watching you two debate the owner of the lucky finger, I should clarify … It's one finger each.

JAYMA / SONNY: Ah fuck!

WOODSY: See ya later, boys.

JAYMA: I can't even see the cow, let alone its ringhole.

GORBY: Use your phone to illuminate the prostate.

EVERYONE: [*not* JAYMA *or* SONNY] ILLUMINATE THE PROSTATE, ILLUMINATE THE PROSTATE, ILLUMINATE THE PROSTATE!

SONNY: Wait, prostate? Is it a cow or a bull?

GJ: Does it matter?

JAYMA: Yes, it matters!

APPLES: I didn't pick you boys as the homophobic types.

SONNY: We ain't homophobic, we're scared.

WOODSY: Scared you'll like it?!

JAYMA: No, fuck ya! Scared the bull's going to object to our fingers being up its arse and then it stomps on our black heads.

JOE: Don't give it a chance to object. Make it want more. Really work that finger.

APPLES: Stroke that prostate, like you're stroking a kitten's ear.

GORBY: Make that kitten purr.

GJ: Meow.

JAYMA: We can do this. Marngrook cousins!

SONNY: Marngrook cousins!

> *They fist pump.*

EVERYONE: [*not* JAYMA *or* SONNY] FINGER IN THE BOVINE SPHINCTER! FINGER IN THE BOVINE SPHINCTER! FINGER IN THE BOVINE SPHINCTER!

> JAYMA *and* SONNY *leave to go stick a finger each up a bull's anus.*

GJ: They'll be okay, right?

JOE: That bull's had so many fingers up its arse over the years, it won't feel a thing.

> EVERYONE *laughs.*

DAZZA: They might be knotty, but Sonny's fingers are only tiny.

EVERYONE *laughs.*

WOODSY: And let's face it, the bull won't see those two coming in the dark.

Silence.

JOE: They're bloody good sports though.

EVERYONE ELSE: Absolutely!

GORBY: You know, I've never really been around an Aboriginal before. They're just like us really.

APPLES: Wow, Gorby, sometimes you amaze me with your wisdom.

GORBY: I was just saying.

JOE: And fuck me, they can play footy.

ANT: I've never seen anyone move like that Jayma, his totem must be a cat.

GJ: Yeah, I don't think it works like that.

JOE: That Sonny is pretty special too. Have you seen his vertical leap? I swear he could do a standing jump over our heads. It's off the show.

GORBY: And they don't go stupid on the alcohol.

JOE: GORBY!

GORBY: What? I just noticed they don't go stupid on the grog. 'Cause I know that some Aboriginals do go stupid on the grog. I'm not judging, I'm just pointing out that our two don't.

APPLES: Fuck me, you are truly exceptional, Gorby.

GORBY: Alright, lay off with the dumb shit, bruv! Not all of us went to a private school.

APPLES: Believe me, one thing you *do not* learn at private school is … how NOT to be an ignorant arsehole.

GORBY: But you learn more education.

APPLES: Argh!

ANT: What's all this 'marngrook cousin' stuff?

APPLES: Marngrook is basically traditional Aboriginal footy.

WOODSY: It's nothing like footy.

APPLES: It is, it's where AFL was derived from.

WOODSY: There's no evidence to support your theory, Apples.

APPLES: Yes, there is. The inventor of AFL grew up in the Grampians and watched the local mob play marngrook. The mark, the kick, it's all marngrook.

WOODSY: All a coincidence, mate. You don't bury the fucken ball in AFL do you?

ANT: I'll bury my balls in your mouth.

APPLES: It's not coincidental, it's factual evidence.

WOODSY: Circumstantial at best, bruv.

DAZZA: Talk about facts, I know for a fact that Sonny and Jayma are already getting paid overs, *and* on four-year contracts, at the request of the General.

WOODSY: Four years?

DAZZA: Yep.

WOODSY: They haven't even played a game yet.

GJ: The General is frothing hard.

ANT: Is Sonny getting the same deal?

DAZZA: Yep.

JOE: It's none of our business, boys, and, Dazza, as a board member, you shouldn't be sharing that information with everyone.

DAZZA: I was just saying.

GORBY: Where are they?

ANT: Hope they're not lost.

GORBY: Aboriginals don't get lost.

EVERYONE: Gorby!

GORBY: What?

BULL: [*offstage*] Moo!

> *Laughs.*

JOE: Wait for it …

BULL: [*offstage*] Moo!

> *Both* JAYMA *and* SONNY *arrive back at the group in a hurry and short of breath.*

JOE: How'd yas go?

ANT: Did you get your fingers right up there?

JAYMA: Yes, they were right up there alright.

JOE: Gorby, smell their fingers.

SONNY / JAYMA: I don't think that's necessary.

JOE: You could say it's Currawong lore, the fingers must be smelt.

EVERYONE: THE FINGERS MUST BE SMELT, THE FINGERS MUST BE SMELT, THE FINGERS MUST BE SMELT.

GORBY *smells their fingers.*

GORBY: That is one hundred percent agricultural!

EVERYONE *cheers.*

JOE: Congratulations, marngrook cousins, you are now Cutting Cove Currawongs.

From the bottom of our hearts, lads: Welcome to the family!

EVERYONE *cheers, and welcome the two new Cove boys into the fold with head rubs and rib-rollers.*

SCENE SIX: THE GENERAL'S TREASURE

Pre-season camp.

THE GENERAL *and* DAZZA *are waiting with stopwatches at the ready. The* TEAM, *with* JOE *and* JAYMA *heading the line, enter running, and then fall to the ground with exhaustion.*

THE GENERAL: Congratulations, boys! Personal best times for each of you!

EVERYONE *cheers.*

What a difference hard work can make, right? I'm proud of you all!

Now, I know you're feeling exhausted, I know you're hurting, and I know you're probably questioning why. Why am I spending time in the hot February sun doing burpees, doing planks and running up godforsaken sand dunes, when I could be chasing girls in bikinis on the beach? I can tell you why, but you're going to have to use your imagination to understand why. Because the riches I'm about to speak of, are so sweet, so shiny, so satisfying, that there isn't a physical example I can use to describe them. These are the treasures that can only be felt in here, in your heart. Some believe the Premiership cup is the treasure, but it's not. Don't get me wrong, the cup is a beauty to behold. And she has a way of making any liquid drank from her edges taste like an angel pissed on your tonsils, but she's not the real treasure.

The real treasure is the feeling when the siren goes and you realise you're now a premiership team. The real treasure is the feeling when you look at the teammate beside you and you both realise you're premiership players. The real treasure is seeing the tears of joy flowing from the supporters' eyes when you hold that cup aloft. The real treasure is going into the pub and the barman says, 'This one's on me, champ, you're a premiership player.' But nothing is for free. Everything has a price. And the things that bring the biggest rewards, have the biggest price tags attached to them. But trust me …

THE GENERAL *pulls out the premiership medallion from his pocket.*

These are worth every push up, every burpee, every sand dune charge, and more. And when I say more, I mean more, because you're gonna have to pay more than February pain for one of these. [*Holding medal in the air*] But that pain is a bloody good deposit. And you can't get a chance at a flag without a February deposit. There's a saying that's as true as your old man's belt strap: 'Premierships aren't won in the pre-season, but they sure as hell can be lost in them.' Let's work, let's pay our February deposit. And let's give ourselves the best chance to grab that treasure when September comes. Do we want it?

TEAM: [*roaring*] Yes!

THE GENERAL: Do you want that treasure?

TEAM: [*roaring*] Yes!

THE GENERAL: It's sitting on top of that sand dune, show me how much you're prepared to work for it. Charge!

TEAM: CHARGE!!!

The screaming players charge up the sand dune and offstage.

DAZZA: They look hungry.

THE GENERAL: Let's hope we can keep them that way, Dazza.

SCENE SEVEN: BONDING TIME

It's the last night of the pre-season camp. DAZZA *is wearing a Currawong puppet on his hand.*

DAZZA: Okay, men, it's that time of pre-season camp that we all love. The time for us to share a little. The time for us to get to know one another. The time for us to get that little bit closer. Men, let the bonding games begin!

Groans.

You're not fooling me, boys, I know you love it. Now, in this bag, there are two coloured bottle caps. If you're lucky enough to pull out a green bottle cap you have to share two lies and a truth, and the rest of us have to figure out which one is the truth. And if you pull out a red bottle cap, you have to share something on the negative side and we have to find a positive spin on it. Are we excited, men?

GORBY: Fucken pumped, Dazza.

DAZZA: Good, Gorby, because you're up first.

GORBY: Fuck no, choose someone else.

DAZZA: Eenie meenie miney mo, catch a—

SONNY: I'll go first.

DAZZA: Good work, Sonny. Jump up, throw your hand in the bag.

SONNY *puts his hand in the bag and pulls out a green bottle cap.*

Green! Okay, so two lies and a truth. The floor is yours, Sonny. Jayma, no word from you.

SONNY: Um, Cathy Freeman is my cousin. I can swim butterfly stroke. And I was born in Taiwan.

JOE: Alright, what do we think, fellas?

ANT: He was telling me earlier that he loves swimming.

APPLES: I love swimming, but I can't swim butterfly.

GJ: No one can, that's why it's special enough to share.

GORBY: He's related to Cathy Freeman?

JOE: You have some inside info?

GORBY: Nah, but aren't most Aboriginals related?

APPLES: I'm pretty sure that's racist, dude?

WOODSY: [*sotto*] Fuck me.

GORBY: Nah, it's not racist. Well, I didn't mean for it to be racist. It's not racist, is it?

JOE: I don't think it is, but I'm just the captain of a footy team and I'm not a racism expert.

WOODSY: It's not racist.

ANT: It's only an observation.

JOE: Either way, I do know that not all Aboriginals are related. So if that's all you have to go on …

GORBY: Yeah, that was it.

GJ: He was born in Taiwan.

JOE: Why do you say that, Junior?

GJ: I just think you'd have to have been there for it to be in your stream of consciousness.

JOE: He could have been on a holiday?

WOODSY: And do you reckon he has a passport?

GORBY: Why wouldn't he have a passport?

WOODSY: Do you have a passport, Gorby?

GORBY: As if, I'm lucky to go past the bridge out of town.

ANT: I've got a passport.

DAZZA: That's because you're wog and half your family live in Greece.

ANT: Italy. Italy! I'm Italian!

WOODSY: Okay, how many other lads have been overseas with their parents?

APPLES: I have.

GORBY: That's 'cause your family are loaded abalone divers, bruv.

APPLES: Who worked bloody hard for our money.

GORBY: Are you saying my family don't work hard, Apples? My nan worked twelve-hour shifts, six days a week, at the meatworks to put food on the table for me and my brother.

JOE: Ladies, calm! Right, so how many of us here and only two of us have parents that took us overseas.

GJ: Perhaps Aboriginal people are more likely to go bush, for their holidays. You know, stay connected with their home country. That's not racist is it?

> *They all look at* JOE.

JOE: Stop looking at me!

ANT: How do we know that Sonny's mum wasn't a dancer for Bangarra and while they happened to be touring over there baby Sonny was shaken loose prematurely from all the dancing?

APPLES: And with a belly full of baby Sonny, she's dancing around Asia with the Bangarra Dance Company?

ANT: It was a theory.

DAZZA: Okay, boys. Which one is the truth?

> *The group, not confident, look at* JOE.

JOE: Cathy Freeman is his cousin.

DAZZA: Sonny?

SONNY: I was born in Taiwan.

My dad was a rigger and was working on an oil rig over there when I was born.

APPLES: Can you speak Mandarin?

SONNY: I was only there for two months.

GORBY: I can speak kiwi fruit. [*Bad Aotearoa accent*] 'Hey bro, look at my big deck.'

EVERYONE *laughs.*

DAZZA: Okay, Joe, you're up.

JOE: Really?

DAZZA *hands* JOE *the bag, suggesting for him to put his hand in.*

JOE *puts his hand in the bag and pulls out a green bottle cap. He shows everyone.*

DAZZA: Another green!

JOE: On my first date with my beautiful wife Lily—I either threw up on her, I shat my pants …

Or I choked on my cheeseburger and coughed up the gherkin … and it landed clean on her face and then slid down her cheek and landed in her drink … plop.

APPLES: How did I know this was going to be about Lily?

GJ: Just because you have commitment issues, Apples.

ANT: I reckon he shat himself.

WOODSY: Same, his farts sound—

GORBY: —Wet

GJ: Tsunami wet.

ANT: There's definitely follow-through happening.

APPLES: But how would he have picked up a second date if he had shat himself?

GJ: I'm surprised he got himself a second date with any of those three scenarios.

JAYMA: I don't think it was the gherkin …

SONNY: Yeah, Macca's cups have lids.

JAYMA: That's it, cuz.

WOODSY: So that leaves us with him spewing on her.

GORBY: Of course, he's shocken for having a spit when he's had a gutfull.

WOODSY: Yep, he's taken her somewhere fancy.

ANT: He was nervous.

JAYMA: Drank too much.

GORBY: And chucked all over her.

SONNY: Nah, just on her feet.

APPLES: Otherwise he wouldn't have picked up that second date if it was all over her favourite dress.

JAYMA: Fuck we're good!

DAZZA: Time's up, you men. Which one is the truth?

ANT: He threw up on poor Lily.

DAZZA: Joe?

JOE: True.

The boys cheer.

THE GENERAL: C'mon, elaborate, Captain.

JOE: I needed some Dutch courage so I started drinking the flask of whiskey I may have had in my pocket and before you know it, I'm telling her that I love her, that I loved her ever since I saw her and then I threw up on her shoes.

WOODSY: Classy cunt you are!

DAZZA: Okay. Jayma, come up here, buddy, and throw your hand in the bag.

JAYMA: No, no, no.

DAZZA: Men?

EVERYONE: JAYMA! JAYMA! JAYMA! JAYMA! JAYMA! JAYMA! JAYMA! JAYMA! JAYMA!

JAYMA *puts his hand in the bag and pulls out a red bottle cap.*

DAZZA: Ohhh … Jayma's pulled a red bottle cap out, men, which means he has to share something on the negative side and we have to find a positive spin on it.

GORBY: Juicy.

JAYMA: My father killed himself when I was ten. Shot himself with a sawn-off shotgun.

DAZZA: Okay, men, how can we find a positive spin on this?

Silence.

WOODSY: It's one less Abo on Centrelink.

JAYMA *charges at* WOODSY *but* SONNY *manages to stop* JAYMA *from getting to him.* JAYMA *is hysterical.*

JAYMA: I'll rip your fucken head off, ya dog cunt!

WOODSY: Calm down, mate, it was just a joke.

JOE: Shut up, Woodsy, just shut up!

JAYMA: I'll give you a joke, you maggot!

SONNY: JAYMA! Calm, cuz.

ANT: Take him that way, Sonny, and I'll take this idiot this way.

> *Both players are escorted off in different directions.*

> DAZZA, JOE *and* THE GENERAL *remain.*

DAZZA: That shitstorm brew up from nowhere.

JOE: Wasn't out of nowhere, Woodsy's a racist turd and he always has been.

DAZZA: Hold up before you brand him with names that stick like that.

JOE: What? You heard him, Dazza. He's fucken racist.

DAZZA: It was tasteless, but was it racist? And, surely it takes more than one silly comment before you're marked a racist.

JOE: One comment? Come on, Dazza, you can hear a dog fart from six mile away, and you've heard the way he bangs on about Asians and—

DAZZA: He makes a solid point though. China basically does own this country.

> And they cannot drive. I should know, I'm a cab driver.

JOE: Dazza, mate, he came to last year's mad Monday dressed as Shaft remember? Complete with black face and a piece of black poly pipe tied between his legs.

DAZZA: Heavens to Betsy, don't tell me that was racist. Shaft was black, and he had a large black shaft on him. Hence the name Shaft.

JOE: Are you kidding me?

THE GENERAL: Dazza, Joe's right. What Woodsy said was racist.

JOE: Thank you. He needs to go.

DAZZA: No, Joe, he made a mistake. You don't throw a bloke out for making a mistake. That would be the epitome of that toxic and baneful trend … cancel culture. That would be cancel culture!

JOE: We can't tolerate that crap, Dazza.

> *Beat.*

DAZZA: And do you think ruck rovers like Woodsy grow on trees?

JOE: Doesn't matter how good of a footy player he is.

DAZZA: It kinda does, mate.

JOE: No it doesn't, mate.

THE GENERAL: It does if we want to salute at the end of the year, Joe.

JOE: Is he really that important to our structures?

THE GENERAL: You know the answer to that. And besides, we don't leave a soldier to the wolves, Captain. If a soldier's injured, we pick him up and help him.

DAZZA: Exactly.

THE GENERAL: Let's get him in, sit him down and look him fair in the eye and explain that racism won't be tolerated at this football club. And we'll send him to one of those cultural awareness courses that Dazza and I did last year.

DAZZA: Great idea, General, that was a magnificent course.

THE GENERAL: Shut up, Dazza!

But first, we'll get him to apologise to Jayma and Sonny. What do you think?

JOE: I think he's past helping.

THE GENERAL: You might be right, son, but it wouldn't sit right with me if we didn't try and help him.

SCENE EIGHT: STRIPPERS AND COKE

JAYMA *and* SONNY *have found a quiet space at the club.* JAYMA *can't sit still. He's pacing.*

JAYMA: That weak-gutted piece of shit. Dad was a better man than that fucken maggot will ever be.

SONNY: He's a wanker, stop giving him any more of your energy.

JAYMA: Did you hear what he said?

SONNY: Yes.

JAYMA: I thought you'd be wanting to smack that cunt and go home.

SONNY: Why, he's a loudmouth, a kookaburra. Who listens to the kookaburra? Not the warrior. And you're a warrior, little cuz.

Enter JOE.

JOE: I'm extremely sorry, boys, that behaviour is not a true reflection of this football club.

Woodsy's having a new arsehole ripped for him right as we speak.

SONNY: Maybe he should be made to do a cultural awareness course.

JOE: We just discussed that and he's not allowed back into the club until he does one.

SONNY: Good!

JOE: [*to* JAYMA] You okay, mate?

JAYMA: Yeah, I'm good.

JOE: I truly am sorry.

> JOE *reaches out to shake hands,* JAYMA *accepts his gesture and shakes his hand.*

JAYMA: Thanks.

JOE: How about you boys come back to the house for a few beers and a feed. My wife Lily and I, we do a mean BBQ. What do you reckon?

SONNY: You had me at beers.

JOE: Jayma?

JAYMA: You had me at feed.

JOE: Brilliant! Are you boys on to those craft beers?

JAYMA / SONNY: Fuck no.

JOE: [*embarrassed*] Me either.

SCENE NINE: LAST GAME OF THE REGULAR SEASON—GAME

The Currawongs' home ground.

There is game in full swing. The Cutting Cove boys are fair in the midst of it, they are playing the Larapuna Mountain Tigers. The crowd is making a ruckus.

EVERYONE: BLACK WHITE WE'RE ALRIGHT, BLACK WHITE WE'RE ALRIGHT, BLACK WHITE WE'RE ALRIGHT, BLACK WHITE WE'RE ALRIGHT.

> *Players shuffle for better position.* JAYMA *takes a mark.*
>
> *He lines up for goal. As he walks back to take his kick.* THE GENERAL *yells out.*

THE GENERAL: TWO MINUTES LEFT, TWO POINTS UP, BUILD THE WALL.

JOE: TWO MINUTES LEFT, TWO POINTS UP, BUILD THE WALL, BUILD THE WALL.

EVERYONE: TWO MINUTES LEFT, TWO POINTS UP, BUILD THE WALL, BUILD THE WALL.

The Currawong players get into their positions and build the wall.

The opposition player who is on the mark is jumping around like a jack jumper, in an attempt to put JAYMA *off his kick for goal.*

OPPOSITION PLAYER ON THE MARK: Aye, aye, look at that fucken mullet. It's as filthy as the dreadlocks hanging from your mum's arse.

JAYMA *kicks the goal.* JOE *runs straight up to the opposition player who made the unsavoury comments and bowls him over with a chest front. He stands over him for a second but is then tackled to the ground by group of opposition players.* JAYMA *comes to his captain's rescue. They all wrestle aggressively. The siren sounds. They all jump up, shake hands and walk off.*

SCENE TEN: LAST GAME OF THE REGULAR SEASON—POST-GAME

Footy sheds.

This scene is a continuation of the last. It's played out in the sheds.

JAYMA *and* JOE *have their arms around each other.*

There's plenty of slaps on the backs, cheering and inaudible shit-talking. It morphs into the club song.

Drink bottles are squirted, there's plenty of arse-smacking, groping and digits searching for holes to 'jokingly' prod.

ALL: [*singing*]
We are the boys of the old black Jays, fighting side by side.
Shoulder to shoulder is how we play the game; fight till we take the prize.
Come and try us at our home, or face us when we roam.
We are the boys of the old black Jays; we'll make it known.
Up your guts, we'll fuck you up, time and time again.
Win and win, we'll take the cup, time and time again.

Ready and strong, marching along, we're the boys of the old black Jays!

THE GENERAL: Are you lot actually happy with that win? I hope not, because that shit's not going to get us far into the finals. What, you think because we finished top of the ladder that means something? What are you smiling at, Apples?

Silence.

That was a piss-weak effort. PISS-WEAK! I've seen more heart at a Wiggles concert. Those derelicts finished second last on the ladder and we beat them by a lousy eight points. PISS-WEAK! You should have chewed those poor bastards up and shat them out tomorrow morning with your morning shit.

You're all here celebrating and I'm thinking Christ, we're a mile off where we should be.

Twenty games down and you'd swear nobody knows what our game plan is, it's like I'm speaking to a brick wall. The home and away season is finished, how can you lot not understand our structures? I'm flabbergasted. I'm at a complete friggen loss.

GJ: We do know the structures, we ju—

THE GENERAL: [*screaming*] If you know them, why do I have to yell at your thick skulls every friggen week about structure, Junior?

Who thinks their spot in this side is safe? Somebody put up your hand, I dare you. 'Cause if you do I'll shove it back up your own arse. That's if it will fit, because obviously your big heads are already up there. And it's got me stuffed why? Because we haven't achieved anything yet. Nothing. Not one bloody thing.

Beat.

I saw one sign of heart out there today. One! Jayma, stand up, son.

JAYMA *stands up.*

Have a look at him. Still shitting yellow. And yet this fella has more heart than the lot of you put together. Your captain is getting beat up by the opposition and what do you lot do?

You pulled up a chair, grabbed some popcorn and watched.

But not Jayma, Jayma went when it was his turn. Jayma put his body on the line for his team when it was his turn. Not one other player put their body on the line today and went when it was their turn. Aside from Jayma.

He knew it was his turn and he went. Because nothing else mattered to him. Not his hair, Apples. Not his safety, Dazza, not his best and fairest votes, Woodsy. Nothing but the defence of his captain, his mate, his fellow soldier. Actually, Jayma, you can put up your hand.

JAYMA *hesitates.*

Go on, right up. Because your position in the side is safe. But the rest of you soft bastards better show me something at training this week or you'll be running water in the semi-final, not playing in the thing.

Silence.

Now shower up and we'll meet in the club rooms ... and forget about that horror show on display out there today.

EVERYONE: Yes, General.

DAZZA: General, I'd appreciate it if you didn't make disparaging remarks in regards to my bravery in front of the players. I'm a board member of this club, which means I'm a leader of this club. And I expect to be treated like one.

THE GENERAL: Well, Dazza, if you expect to be treated like a leader, step up.

DAZZA: Fair enough.

They shake hands.

SCENE ELEVEN: LET IT GO

A continuation from the last scene.

Everyone else has left, leaving JAYMA*,* JOE *and* SONNY *alone in the sheds.* SONNY *is busy texting on his phone.*

JOE: Thanks for having my back out there today, man.

JAYMA: All good, brah, that's what we do right?

JOE: Too right, mate.

They shake hands.

JAYMA: Anyways, you defended the honour of my mother's arse hairs. It was the least I could do.

JOE: I'd hope you'd do it for mine.

JAYMA: Brus, they're undefendable. That's that Tassie old-growth forest stuff there.

> JOE *and* JAYMA *laugh.*

> SONNY *puts his phone in his bag and joins* JAYMA *and* JOE.

SONNY: Guess who just got a free pass for the night off their woman?

JAYMA: Who?

SONNY: Me!

> *They do an excited dance.*

JAYMA: How'd you manage that?

SONNY: Because when the kids got full bellies and clothes on their backs, Mama Bear loves Papa Bear.

JAYMA: Well, the marngrook cuzzies are on the frothies tonight! [*To* JOE] You sinking a few with us, brah?

JOE: Nah, Lily's going out with a few of her mates which leaves me and the kids free for a movie night.

SONNY: What are you watching?

JOE: *The Lego Movie.*

SONNY: Awesome.

> SONNY *and* JOE *sing 'Everything Is AWESOME!!!' from* The Lego Movie.

> *They fist pump.*

I'll see you at the bar, cunts. Gorby!

> SONNY *leaves, chasing* GORBY *with a coiled towel to whip him.* JOE *hands a card to* JAYMA.

JAYMA: What's this?

JOE: It's a little thank-you from Lily and the kids for going in to speak to her class last week, she said it was the best NAIDOC week they've ever had. The kids are still talking about it.

JAYMA: Ah fuck yeah, that's deadly.

JOE: Oh, and she said the teacher's aid really really really appreciated you!

JAYMA: Nope, I'm not going there.

JOE: Once they go black they never go back, isn't that what you say?

JAYMA: Yeah, but once you go hungry white women in her thirties, you die.

    JOE *and* JAYMA *laugh.*

SCENE TWELVE: SPEARING A CHEER SQUAD

Clubhouse.

The TEAM *is celebrating in the clubhouse, watching footy on the club room TV.* SONNY *grabs a beer and joins them.*

EVERYONE: [*at the TV screen*] BALL!

ANT: That's fucken bullshit! He's held it longer than a Whitney Houston note.

GORBY: Who you going for tonight, General??

THE GENERAL: I'm not fazed, Gorby. I haven't supported anyone since my beloved Fitzroy Lions folded.

SONNY: Who?

DAZZA: I hope Carlton rips the wings off those fudge-packing Swans.

SONNY: Well you're shit out of luck, Dazza, 'cause the Swans are flying tonight, brah.

THE GENERAL: Why are the Swans on song tonight, Sonny?

SONNY: 'Cause they are?

THE GENERAL: Think about it, why is their game strong tonight?

SONNY: Awesome team defence.

THE GENERAL: Sorry, what defence?

SONNY: Team defence.

THE GENERAL: So, no 'me-me-me' stuff?

SONNY: Ha, nah, brah.

THE GENERAL: No marngrook.

SONNY: No marngrook.

THE GENERAL: Just the team game.

SONNY: Yep.

THE GENERAL: Mmmm.

APPLES: Adam Goodes has it on a string tonight.

GJ: He's a wanker, that bloke.

ANT: He's an all-time tosspot.

APPLES: He's a two-time Brownlow medallist.

GORBY: But a bit of a bully, picking on that thirteen-year-old girl like he did.

APPLES: She was screaming racist abuse at him over the fence.

DAZZA: And?

Come and hear what is said to me in my cab on a Friday night. Sticks and stones, my friend.

GORBY: What do you think of Goodesy, Sonny?

APPLES: Yeah put the First Nations person on the spot why don't you, Gorby!

GORBY: I just thought I'd ask, leave me alone, dickhead.

DAZZA: I can honestly say, that my dislike for him isn't racially motivated. I dislike him because he's a sook. And the constant diving for free kicks drives me insane!

GJ: Playing the victim.

ANT: He's always the victim, that Adam Goodes. Poor Adam doesn't get a free kick, poor Adam gets called nasty names, poor Adam gets booed.

DAZZA: You're quiet, Woodsy.

WOODSY *mimes zipping his mouth shut.*

Enter JAYMA *and* JOE.

APPLES: Look who has finally graced us with their presence. Our fearless leader and our star attraction. The sweet alliteration of Joe and Jayma.

Applause.

JOE: Thank you for that wonderful introduction, Apples. You feel special, Jayma?

JAYMA: Absolutely.

JAYMA *looks up at the footy on the TV.*

C'mon on, the Swannies!

THE GENERAL: You a Swans lad, Jayma?

JAYMA: Sure am, General! Goodesy's my boy. Love the brother.

They all look at JAYMA.

EVERYONE: [*at the TV screen*] IN THE BACK!

THE GENERAL: [*to* JOE] What did you get up to today, Joe?

JOE: What do you mean?

THE GENERAL: I'm just wondering what you got up to today?

JOE: I played footy.

THE GENERAL: Oh, really, who for?

JOE: [*catching on*] I know, I didn't have the best game today.

EVERYONE: [*at the TV screen*] DELIBERATE!

JOE: Anyway, I better head off.

DAZZA: Who's heading off?

JOE: Me.

DAZZA: Hear that, lads, our captain's departing the ship early.

EVERYONE: BOOOOOO!

GORBY: Why?

JOE: 'Cause I have shit to do.

ANT: 'Shit to do', mate, you're as soft as Apples' hair.

GJ: As soft as Dazza's tits.

GORBY: As soft as erectile dysfunction.

APPLES: You halfwit!

GORBY: Call me a halfwit one more time and I swear—

> JOE *intervenes and hands his beer to* GORBY.

JOE: I know, I'm as weak as piss. I'll CATCH YA FELLAS LATER!

EVERYONE: [*at* JOE] BOOOOOOO!!!

JAYMA: [*at the TV screen*] Psssss!!! Adam Goodes, you fucken gun!

SONNY: [*to* JAYMA] Hey, cuz, have I been playing alright? Be honest.

JAYMA: Knock off, tuck, you're carving it up. You're the second-best player in the team.

SONNY: Ha! It's the best I've played in years.

> We could do something special here.

JAYMA: I know.

EVERYONE: [*at the TV screen*] ON THE FULL!

DAZZA: [*spruiking*] Meat raffle, get your tickets for the meat raffle here, ladies and buffoons. Meat raffle, meat raffle!

APPLES: And what do we have in the meat raffle, Dazza from K'nazza?

DAZZA: I'm glad you asked, Apples from K'napples.

> We have an array of gourmet here.

> We got beef snags. Pork snags, and [*pointing towards some players*] any of those slags.

And don't forget the lamb. This country was built on a sheep's back! And so is this meat tray.

We got chops, and cutlets and a roast … this really is the meat tray with the most.

Okay, two dollars a ticket or two for five. Throw your money in the tin and be prepared to win. And then … let HAPPY HOUR BEGIN!

He shakes the tin.

ALL: [*singing*]

> Played all his game on the wing wing wing,
> He's a good fella he is, he is, he is.
> Ran and ran and ran but didn't touch the ball.
> Sacrificed his game when the coach made the call.
> Now they celebrate their winny win win,
> With beer dripping from their chinny chin chins.

EVERYONE *breaks into a stylised slow-motion montage. They are messy drunk. Sculling beers, dancing with one another, re-enacting lewd sex acts on one another.* GORBY *passes out and they take turns in violating him whilst he's unconscious. Only breaking out of the slow motion three separate times during the montage to scream 'BALL', 'WHAT A GRAB', 'COME ON UMPIRE' respectively.*

Break out of montage.

APPLES: And you have to admit. I'm the best-looking apple in this apple cart.

ANT: Get him out of here.

APPLES: Serious, look at me. Look at the guns on him, look at the pins. I'm a gift from the heavens to the women of Cutting Cove.

GJ: Jayma shits all over you in the looks department.

APPLES: SAYS YOU! Who has a biased taste for chocolate.

GJ: So what if I like my meat seared first?

> GJ *grabs hold of* JAYMA, THE GENERAL *watches on in disgust.*

I mean look at this fella, will you. Big beautiful dark eyes, olive complexion, and hung like a donkey. I mean who in their right mind would choose your little white pale arse and pin dick over this divine creature? I mean, can I get me an amen, people.

EVERYONE: AMEN!

APPLES: Whatever, fuckwits!

THE GENERAL: Alright, men, I'm off.

DAZZA: Mrs General must be getting worried, General.

THE GENERAL: Yes, Dazza, Mrs General would be waiting up for me I'd say.

GORBY: She'll be waiting up alright, she'll be waiting for the General's big blue vein pumper! [*Pelvic thrusting*] Yes, yes, yes, alpha charlie fire that cannon, General!!!!

THE GENERAL *gets in* GORBY*'s face.*

THE GENERAL: You don't talk about my wife like that, okay.

GORBY: Yeah, bruv.

THE GENERAL: You don't talk about my wife like that.

GORBY: I was only joking.

THE GENERAL *grabs* GORBY *by the chest.*

THE GENERAL: YOU DON'T TALK ABOUT MY WIFE LIKE THAT!

GORBY: I'm sorry.

THE GENERAL *lets him go. Pats him on the head.*

THE GENERAL: What would your *nan* say?

Night, men.

TEAM: Night, General.

THE GENERAL *leaves.*

During this next bit, the laughing gets louder with every euphemism for a beating.

APPLES: Gorby nearly got his arse kicked.

DAZZA: Old-man beat-down.

WOODSY: Wiped the floor with.

ANT: Dropped.

SONNY: Possum stomped.

DAZZA: Teeth kicked in.

APPLES: Smokey Joe KO'd.

ANT: Owned!

SONNY: Knocked the fuck out!

GORBY *is now smoking-ears angry.*

EVERYONE *stops laughing,* SONNY *doesn't notice and keeps laughing.*

GORBY: [*to* SONNY] What are you laughing at, mate?

JAYMA (*as Adam Goodes*) *replicates the famous Adam Goodes war dance and spear throw into the crowd/audience* (*which happened during this game*).

DAZZA: Did Adam Goodes just pretend to throw a spear into the crowd?

ANT: No way?

DAZZA: Yes way!

GORBY: I'm not sure how I feel about that.

GJ: Me either, mate.

APPLES: I thought it was super powerful!

GJ: What was that?

WOODSY: It was pretty obvious what it was.

WOODSY *zips his mouth.*

ANT: That was a fucken threat. That's what it was.

DAZZA: If I was in that crowd with my kid, I would leap that fence and stick the spear up his proverbial.

GORBY: Not with those hamstrings, Dazza.

EVERYONE *laughs.*

JAYMA: That'd hurt, sticking a pretend spear up the arse.

Silence.

WOODSY: Just imagine …

JAYMA: Imagine what, Woodsy?

WOODSY *makes a gesture to zip his mouth.*

GJ: What if Patrick Dangerfield pretended to shoot Aboriginal people in the crowd. How would that go down with your mob, Jayma?

DAZZA: Yeah, that's a good point, GJ!

JAYMA: Fuck off, are you really butt hurt because Goodesy pretended to throw a spear into the Carlton cheer squad?

GORBY: What if Dangerfield had done what GJ said though?

JAYMA: Then it'd be different because we don't have the history of shooting you fellas … you hearing me??

GORBY: Yeah, yeah, I hear ya. I think.

WOODSY: No history of white man being killed by a black man, Jayma, I think you'll find on my family's property two white men were speared to death. Both speared to death through their white necks by black men whilst they grazed their flock.

I'll shut up now.

JAYMA: Why, because you're a racist and you can't control it?

WOODSY: See …

DAZZA: Jayma, he attended the culture course.

WOODSY: Doesn't matter, mate—

DAZZA: It does matter, mate. The penance has been paid and it's not fair that he keeps holding what was said months ago against you.

ANT: What do you reckon, Sonny?

SONNY: About what?

WOODSY: Goodes doing what he did. It's racist, isn't it.

SONNY: I guess it could be perceived that way.

WOODSY: See, even your own mob thinks it's racist, son.

JAYMA: Are you having a laugh, cuz?

WOODSY: He's allowed to have a voice of his own, mate.

JAYMA: Shut the fuck up, and go sniff Tony Abbott's budgie smugglers or whatever the fuck you rednecks do for kicks.

WOODSY: You're a proper fuckwit, aren't you.

JAYMA *and* WOODSY *lock eyes.*

DAZZA: C'mon, boys, there's been an apology. We now need to move on. For the team.

WOODSY: It'll never be enough, mate. Don't stress.

SONNY: Alright, alright, alright. We've said what we wanted to say, now let's just move on and have a beer. Who wants a freshie?

JAYMA: Why are you enabling them, cuz?

SONNY: I'm not enabling anyone, Jayma. I'm just having a beer after a game of footy. That's all I want. I've got a free pass from the missus for the night, I don't wanna waste that golden ticket fighting over politics.

Silence.

DAZZA: And the winner is. Ticket eighty-eight … Jayma.

JAYMA: Stick it up your fucking arse!

JAYMA *leaves.*

DAZZA: Okedoke.

DAZZA *drops his shorts and pretends to stick the ticket up his arse. It breaks the tension and* EVERYONE *eventually begins to laugh.*

ANT *grabs* DAZZA *in a drunken friendly embrace.*

ANT: Dazza, you're a toffee-nose fuck sometimes but you're such a mad cunt! That's why I love ya!

DAZZA: Love you too, my wog friend.

They cuddle and then kick off a club chant.

Cutting Cove are on the go.

EVERYONE: Cutting Cove are on the go.

DAZZA: We're the best and we all know.

EVERYONE: We're the best and we all know.

DAZZA: All the rest are far behind.

EVERYONE: All the rest are far behind.

DAZZA: We're the next premiership side.

EVERYONE: We're the next premiership side.

SCENE THIRTEEN: 37

Training.

APPLES, DAZZA *and* ANT *are stretching. The rest of the boys are yet to arrive.*

SONNY: Boys.

APPLES: Bro, how the fuck did you pull up the other night?

DAZZA: He didn't until Sunday arvo.

SONNY: I can speak for myself, cunt lips.

DAZZA: Don't get aggressive with me, my friend.

ANT: Have you heard from Jayma?

SONNY: Nah.

ANT: I hope he doesn't go MIA like his old man did.

WOODSY: Boys.

EVERYONE: Woodsy.

GJ: How'd you pull up after Saturday night, Woodsy?

WOODSY: Better than Sonny.

SONNY: How would you know?

WOODSY: I ran into you and Gorby on Sunday morning, remember?

SONNY: No.

WOODSY: That doesn't surprise me actually, you were both … um …

ANT: A fucken mess?

WOODSY: As messes go, they were messier than a milkin' shed floor.

Enter GORBY.

GORBY: Fuck off, we were a bigger mess than that. We were a power shit on public toilet wall.

WOODSY: Fair call.

APPLES: You still smell like it too.

GORBY: That's harsh.

DAZZA: [*sniffs*] More like a compliment.

GORBY: Hang on, I might have shit myself.

GORBY *puts a hands down the back of his pants and then pulls it out to see if there's any brown on it.*

Nah, all clear. Must be me training gear. I haven't washed it all season.

Enter JOE.

EVERYONE: Captain.

GORBY: Is Jayma joining us, Skip?

JOE: He didn't say he wasn't when he stopped in home.

SONNY: When did he stop into yours?

JOE: This morning.

GJ: He got pretty worked up about Goodes, didn't he.

SONNY: He's just a young staunch warrior, and young staunch warriors, they fight with their heart.

ANT: Nah, there was no need for it.

JOE: It's over now so don't go on about, aye.

WOODSY: We're not the ones that went on about it.

APPLES: Bullshit.

ANT: We had a fucken opinion, that's all.

DAZZA: And surely we're entitled to an opinion, since it was us, white Australia, that Goodes was throwing a spear at.

ANT: Did you know that it was a war dance he was doing? Saw it on *The Footy Show*.

WOODSY: A declaration of war on white Australia.

APPLES: On the Carlton cheer squad!

WOODSY: Apples, we get it, mate, you wanna suck Goodes' cock.

APPLES: At least I'd get a mouthful, can't say the same for your girlfriend.

ANT: So, you don't stand with your own, Apples … hey, boys?

APPLES: I'm standing with common sense.

WOODSY: He's declaring war on our way of life.

First, he threatens a young white girl because she called him a silly name, then he threatens Aussies just for being here.

APPLES: She called him an ape.

WOODSY: He looks like an ape.

GJ: Woodsy!

WOODSY: He does, not because he's black, because he's got massive ears and how buff the prick is.

APPLES: Bullshit.

WOODSY: Whoopee fucken do, if she called him a name, that's what we do, stir each other … Dazza, you're an ugly fuck.

DAZZA: Who has intercourse with your mother.

EVERYONE *laughs.*

WOODSY: Ant, you're a greasy wog.

ANT: Get fucked, you sheep-fucker.

WOODSY: You weren't offended?

ANT: Nah, mate, and do you know why, boys? Because that is what we do at this footy club. We take the piss out of each other.

GORBY: No it's not, Ant, it's what Woodsy and Dazza do.

APPLES: Spot on, Gorby.

SONNY: Alright, can we talk about something else, fellas, I'm sick of this divisive shit.

WOODSY: Talking about divisive, Goodes wins Australian of the Year and then uses that as a chance to publicly call Australia Day—

WOODSY / DAZZA: —Invasion Day.

WOODSY: That's divisive, mate, is it not?

JAYMA *arrives wearing an Indigenous round Sydney Swans jumper with Adam Goodes' number on the back, 37.*

JAYMA: Lads.

Silence.

How 'Goodes' this arvo, aye? It's the new Sydney Swans jumper, the Indigenous round to be specific. And, GJ, guess whose number I have on the back?

GJ: Adam Goodes.

JAYMA: Fucken good guess.

WOODSY: I'm not training with him while he's wearing that.

JAYMA: Why, do you wanna wear it?

WOODSY: No, I don't want to wear it.

JAYMA: Then what's the problem?

WOODSY: You know what the problem is.
It's what it represents.

JAYMA: What does it represent?

JOE: Woodsy, it's a jumper.

WOODSY: It's more than that, and you know it.

JAYMA: If it's more than that, what is it then?

JOE: Woodsy, it's a jumper.

WOODSY: …

JOE: Jayma, I have nothing against the jumper, you know this, but, brah, can you take it off until training finishes? Just so we can get on with what we came here for … to train.

JAYMA: Not happening, brah.
Hey, Woodsy, you wanna touch my new guernsey?

WOODSY: Piss off.

JAYMA: Come on, touch it, I don't mind.

WOODSY: If you think I'm scared of you, you're in for a rude shock.

JAYMA: Touch the numbers … you know you want to.

WOODSY: You lot wonder why?

JAYMA: Touch the Australian of the Year's jumper, Woodsy.

WOODSY: Keep going, sunshine.

WOODSY *takes a step closer.*

JAYMA: Touch it, 'once you go black, you never go back'.

WOODSY *faux moves his shoulder, as if he's about to throw a punch.* JAYMA *doesn't flinch. They are in each other's faces now.*

Enter THE GENERAL.

THE GENERAL: Have you done your laps?

> *Silence.*

Don't all answer me at once.

GJ: I haven't done mine yet.

THE GENERAL: What are you waiting for? An invitation from the Queen? Anyone else need to run their laps?

> EVERYONE *aside from* WOODSY *gets up and begins to run their laps.* JAYMA *holds for a moment.*

Go!

JAYMA: They reckon red goes faster, General, I might do a PB today in this new jumper.

SONNY: [*to* JAYMA] Hey, warrior, don't forget the marngrook.

JAYMA: You're full of shit.

> JAYMA *begins his lap.*

THE GENERAL: What's this stuff about you not training?

WOODSY: I'm not training with him while he's wearing that jumper.

THE GENERAL: I can't make him take it off, Woodsy. Just ignore him.

WOODSY: I thought we're supposed to be a team, not a group of individuals.

THE GENERAL: He's just blowing off a little steam.

WOODSY: He's causing division and Joe and yourself aren't helping the cause when you let him get away with shit like tonight. Just remember, my family and other sponsors put money into this club.

> WOODSY *runs off.* DAZZA *enters.*

DAZZA: This is escalating and causing division.

THE GENERAL: It's nothing.

DAZZA: You don't want to call a team pow-wow?

THE GENERAL: Why, Dazza, why would I want to bring attention to something that is nothing? Next week the news will be talking about something and Jayma and everyone will have forgotten about Adam Goodes.

DAZZA: Fair enough.

THE GENERAL: Do us a favour will you, and get Jayma to fill up the water bottles.

DAZZA: [*shouting*] Jayma!

SCENE FOURTEEN: PRELIM FINAL—PRE-GAME SPEECH

It's game day, and it's moments before the first siren is sounded. THE
GENERAL *has his* TEAM *bailed up on the side of the ground, giving
them one last talk before they go into battle.*

THE GENERAL: Today the maths is simple, men. We win, we're into a
Grand Final. We lose, we go home with nothing but a full belly of
regret. And, how we win is simple. We play the same game we have
played all year. The same game that got us to this position. And
what game is that?

TEAM: THE TEAM GAME.

THE GENERAL: WHICH MEANS WE HAVE TO SHEPHERD FOR …

TEAM: ONE ANOTHER.

THE GENERAL: CHASE FOR …

TEAM: ONE ANOTHER.

THE GENERAL: GET INTO THE RIGHT SPOTS FOR …

TEAM: ONE ANOTHER.

THE GENERAL: LOOK FOR …

TEAM: ONE ANOTHER.

THE GENERAL: AND WORK FOR …

TEAM: ONE ANOTHER.

THE GENERAL: For one another. We play our team game, keep our
structures, and everything else will fall into place.

Go and get 'em, soldiers.

TEAM: WOO!

SCENE FIFTEEN: PRELIM FINAL—GAME

The PLAYERS *run out and set themselves into their positions.*

This scene, like the other footy scenes, is a stylised dance/movement piece.

*The game begins with the siren and the whistle. The ball is bounced
and the rucks contest the ball.*

The feel is that it's a close game, but the Currawongs are in control.
JAYMA *can't get into it though. His leads are being ignored, shepherds
are not being laid on his behalf, no one is working for him. He is*

rough-handled by the other team but no help is given. JAYMA *becomes angry, which leads to him taking a 'solo approach' when he does get his chances with the ball – which are often met with an opposition hard tackle or mistake from* JAYMA. *Which results in him losing the ball.*

Time passes to the final siren. The Currawongs have won and as a result are through to the Grand Final. They celebrate, patting each other's heads, backs and arses as they walk into the change rooms.

SCENE SIXTEEN: PRELIM FINAL—POST-GAME

They sing the club song, with spirit. JAYMA *is, and feels, very much isolated from the team camaraderie.*

ALL: [*singing*]
> Up your guts, we'll fuck you up, time and time again.
> Win and win, we'll take the cup, time and time again.
> Ready and strong, marching along, we're the boys of the old black Jays!

THE GENERAL: Sonny, come here …

I think that was the most team-orientated game you've played for us. You ran, you chased, you filled holes and you created space. You lowered your eyes and you brought others into the game. Well done, Sonny!

Cheers and applause.

Joe. A great captain's game today, Joe. You've found that old spark and that spark ignites the rest of the team. Take it into next week.

Cheers and applause.

[*Calling*] Woodsy!

TEAM: [*responding*] Woodsy!

THE GENERAL: Rock-solid in the guts today, Woodsy, especially in the second half. You are the glue that bound our midfield and your leadership is growing for all to see. Keep it up, mate. There were lots of other solid contributors out there today, I'm not going to name you all.

Cheers and applause.

Jayma, you were our weak link today, son.

JAYMA: What?! I tried but nobody would share the ball, or shepherd or fucken anything—

THE GENERAL: —No, don't blame anyone else here, don't try to pass the buck, you need to take responsibility.

JAYMA: Ole be fucked, you gotta be kidding me!

THE GENERAL: No, there's no kidding here.

Today you didn't play the team game.

JAYMA: I was left to dry out there. I may as well been playing for the other team. And we all know why …

WOODSY: [*under his breath*] Here we go, it's because he's Aboriginal.

JAYMA: If you're gunna say something, you weak cunt, fucken say it, don't fucken mutter it under your breath.

WOODSY: You're the weak cunt, blaming everything on your Aboriginal heritage, like Goodes.

And just like Goodes, nobody likes you because you're a whinging troublemaking sooky fuck.

JAYMA: Is this right, Joe?

JOE: C'mon, fellas. Calm down.

WOODSY: Answer him, Joe.

GJ: We just won a prelim final, for God's sake.

WOODSY: Sit down, Junior … Joe?

JAYMA: Joe?

JOE: Bruv, you're not hated but you do bring things upon yourself sometimes.

JAYMA: Thanks for the back-up, my brother. Thanks a fucken lot.

JOE: Mate, I love ya, I do, but you just can't leave things be.

WOODSY: Watch out, Joe, the sook will call you a racist next.

JAYMA: [*to* WOODSY] Keep going, you white cunt …

WOODSY: He called me a white cunt, he should have to do a white cultural awareness course.

ANT: Alright, relax.

THE GENERAL: Jayma, go for a walk, son.

JAYMA: I'm not going nowhere.

THE GENERAL: Son, go for a walk.

Silence.

WOODSY: Does anybody else notice we never see Sonny calling us all white cunts or fighting with anybody?

DAZZA: Because he's easygoing, our Sonny.

SONNY: No, because look what happens when you bite back.

You all did leave Jayma to dry out there today, and he's right, it was because the young warrior stood up to you.

WOODSY: 'Warrior', what a joke!

Your people aren't warriors, warriors don't lose. Your people lost to our people and you need to get over it. Simple.

Our biggest mistake was not finishing the job properly!

SONNY *charges at* WOODSY *and begins to lay into him.* EVERYONE *pulls him off* WOODSY, *but the damage is done and* WOODSY *is left bloodied and bruised.*

THE GENERAL: Jesus Christ, take him outside and put the hose on him or something.

JAYMA *and* SONNY *exit one way, and* GORBY *and* ANT *help* WOODSY *off in the opposite direction.*

SCENE SEVENTEEN: WE CAN'T WIN IT WITHOUT THEM

DAZZA, THE GENERAL, JOE, GJ *and* APPLES *are having a meeting in the sheds.*

DAZZA: As a member of the club's board, it's my duty to report this to the rest of the board.

THE GENERAL: No, you're fucken not.

DAZZA: Yes, I fucken am!

Long pause.

I'm stepping up. I can't sit by and watch you let players assault their teammates, no matter what the reason.

JOE: You do that and the board will tear up their contracts and kick them out of the club.

DAZZA: So! We're lucky it wasn't worse. He could have bloody killed him.

THE GENERAL: Dazza, we're a week out from Grand Final and you want to get our two best players kicked out of the club?

DAZZA: You can't assault your teammates and we can't be seen tolerating it. What would the sponsors say, what would the town say?

JOE: Woodsy deserved it though.

GJ: He totally crossed the line.

THE GENERAL: The boys are right. He had it coming, Dazza.

DAZZA: And he may have, but when it comes down to it: which side do you think the town's going to take? A seventh-generation cove boy, or two boys up from the valley?

APPLES: Two Aboriginal boys from up the valley …

DAZZA: I didn't say that.

THE GENERAL: Dazza, do you want a flag?

DAZZA: You know the answer to that.

THE GENERAL: Twenty years ago this club nearly won a flag, remember?

DAZZA: Yeah I remember.

THE GENERAL: And what happened?

DAZZA: Darky Mansell went walkabout.

THE GENERAL: And?

DAZZA: We lost the Grand Final.

THE GENERAL: Well, then listen: you need to trust me when I tell you we can't win on Saturday without Jayma and Sonny on our side.

DAZZA: If we do nothing about the assault, the sponsors in the town will drop us like flies.

THE GENERAL: The truth is, the town wants a flag, mate. I'm sure everyone will be happy to turn a blind eye for a week.

DAZZA: A week? What do you mean, 'a week'?

THE GENERAL: If you have to go to the board, mate, go to the board, but pitch them this: Let Jayma and Sonny play on Saturday *but* don't honour their contracts beyond the Grand Final.

DAZZA: That's a good idea. I could sell that. It's a win-win.

THE GENERAL: A win-win.

APPLES: It's wrong, it's fucken wrong, Sonny and his partner have begun saving for a deposit on a house.

DAZZA: If you're so offended by it, Apples, you can pay their next three years out with your family's abalone money?

Silence.

JOE: General, we don't leave a soldier to the wolves, remember?

THE GENERAL: I have a whole pack to think about, Captain.

APPLES: And they're a massive part of our pack.

THE GENERAL: [*pulling out his medal*] To win these, boys … Sacrifices must be made.

GJ: You and your bloody medal. You know how he got that medal, men?

He played one senior game his whole life … that Grand Final. They brought him up from the reserves to take out the opposition's best player. And he did. Broke his cheekbone, hey, Dad?

THE GENERAL *stares down his son.*

THE GENERAL: AND I WOULDN'T THINK FOR A SECOND TO DO IT AGAIN! BECAUSE I DID IT FOR MY TEAM!

Beat.

Gorby, God bless his cotton socks, but what would a flag do for a guy like Gorby? Ant, how would Ant celebrate for weeks if he got his hands on that cup, how would his community celebrate?

Boys, do you know how close we are, we're this close.

Beat.

Joe, how many years have you been playing footy without a premiership to your name?

JOE: Twenty-five.

THE GENERAL: Twenty-five years of playing in the cold and rain, twenty-five years of injuries. Twenty-five years of brutal hard footy.

And we both know you're slowing down out there, son, this may be the last chance for you …

So you have to ask yourself: what if this happened to be my last game, would I be happy ending it without a flag?

Beat.

We can't think about a couple people here, boys, we have to think about everyone, because the team comes?

EVERYONE: First, second and third.

GJ, APPLES *and* JOE *leave.*

SCENE EIGHTEEN: KMART REMINISCING

JAYMA *and* SONNY *are sitting out on the oval having this conversation.*

JAYMA: Bro, you drove that fuck straight between his eyes.
I thought I'd be the one who'd end up tapping him.
SONNY: You remember that time when we were kids in Kmart?
JAYMA: Yeah, when they blamed us for knocking something off.
SONNY: Fuck, that still pisses me off when I think back to it.
Those arseholes had us stripped down to our undies in front of everyone. All their eyes looking at us like we were the scum of the earth. And we didn't even do a thing.
JAYMA: I just remember sitting there crying me little eyes out.
SONNY: Fuck, brah, if you cried any more, we could've made a swimming escape.
JAYMA: We would've had to knock off some floaties, because I couldn't swim.

Pause.

SONNY: That contract and those match payments have made the world of difference for us back home. For the first time since we bought the fridge, it's been full. The kids have new uniforms. And we're even saving for a house. I heard everything but I was ignoring it.
JAYMA: Sacrificing for the family, brah.
SONNY: I was compromising my values, cuz. But I'm ready to tell them to shove their Grand Final and their contracts up their arses if you are?
JAYMA: The big cods are normally biting in the river this time of year.
SONNY: I could go for a feed of cod.
JAYMA: Me too.
JAYMA / SONNY: Mmmm.
JAYMA: We didn't come this far for nothing.
Fuck these fucks. The warrior doesn't listen to the kookaburra. Let's go out there and carve it up, marngrook style and finish this for Dad!

Long pause.

For the marngrook.
SONNY: For the marngrook.

SCENE NINETEEN: GRAND FINAL—PRE-GAME SPEECH

This scene is situated in the club rooms. It's moments before the Grand Final begins.

EVERYONE: BLACK WHITE WE'RE ALRIGHT, BLACK WHITE WE'RE ALRIGHT, BLACK WHITE WE'RE ALRIGHT.

JOE: Get one last drink into you, fellas. Take a seat.

THE GENERAL: Lads, in life, to get something that you don't already have, chances are you're gunna have to pay a price to get it. Today that's a certainty. Every one of us is going to have to pay a price if we are gunna be drinking that angel piss from the shiny cup in a couple of hours. Now, I can hear some of you say: General, we've been paying, but, boys, we haven't finished paying yet. Because what we want is expensive! It's the most expensive prize in football.

So, I'm asking for two more hours of hard work. Two more hours of working for one another. Two more hours of getting the hard ball.

THE GENERAL *pulls out his premiership medal.*

Are you prepared to pay the price?

TEAM: [*roaring*] Yes!

THE GENERAL: Are you prepared to pay the price for the team?

TEAM: [*roaring*] Yes!

THE GENERAL: Are you prepared to pay the price for greatness!

TEAM: [*roaring*] Yes!

THE GENERAL: When it's your turn to go, what are you gunna do?

TEAM: Go!

THE GENERAL: When it's your turn to go, what are you gunna do?

TEAM: Go!

THE GENERAL: WHEN IT'S YOUR TURN TO GO, WHAT ARE YOU GUNNA FUCKEN DO?

TEAM: GO!

They form a tight circle in the middle.

THE GENERAL: Today's the day, men. Today we become immortals of this club, of this town.

UP THE MIGHTY COVE BOYS!

TEAM: UP THE MIGHTY COVE BOYS!

The TEAM *are amping their fucking chops off as they run out.*
THE GENERAL *stops* JAYMA.

THE GENERAL: Jayma, I know you're hurting, son, but you pay the price today, the holy grail is ours.

JAYMA: What price you paying, General?

SCENE TWENTY: GRAND FINAL—GAME

The Grand Final.

The PLAYERS *are in their positions. It's very tense. Plenty of pushing and shoving. A fight breaks out between* APPLES *and his opponent. It's defused and the siren sounds.*

From the start, it's super-intense and physical. The tackles are harder, the hits are harder, the celebrations are more.

It only intensifies as the game goes on. Quarter after quarter, it's shove-for-shove, tackle-for-tackle, goal-for-goal. JAYMA *and* SONNY *take the game on Marngrook-style. They get the game on the Currawongs' terms. The Currawongs are down by three points, thirty seconds to go in the game ...*

THE GENERAL: Three points down! Thirty seconds left!

... JAYMA *takes a spectacular mark, over multiple players, in front of the Lions' goals.*

The siren sounds!!

The crowd are going nuts.

JAYMA, *taking deep breaths, walks back to his mark.*

He is nervously looking at the goals, lining his kick up.

JOE *and* SONNY *approach.*

JOE: One straight kick, brother, and you win a flag for the Currawongs.

SONNY: Your dad's watching down on you, little cuz. Just let him guide the ball for you.

The opposition have all their players on the mark, and they're jumping up and about crazily in an attempt to put JAYMA *off his kick.*

WOODSY *approaches.*

WOODSY: Kick this, Darky, and you'll be a Cutting Cove Currawong for life.

WOODSY *pats* JAYMA *on the back before jogging off.*

JAYMA *watches* WOODSY *jog off. Then turns to look at the bench. Where* THE GENERAL *is watching on nervously.*

JAYMA *places the ball on the ground, places some dirt over it and then walks off the ground.*

The siren sounds.

THE END

www.ingramcontent.com/pod-product-compliance
Lightning Source LLC
Chambersburg PA
CBHW050025090426
42734CB00021B/3425